ADOPTION

IS A LIFELONG

JOURNEY

ADOPTION IS A LIFELONG JOURNEY

Printed in the United States of America. For information, address
Boston Post Adoption Resources, 235 Cypress Street, Brookline, MA 02445.

www.bpar.org

The information provided in this book is not intended as a substitute for medical care or medical advice. Please consult with a medical care provider regarding any medical questions you may have. Boston Post Adoption Resources (BPAR) and its members, managers, officers, employees, agents and the assigns of the same, disclaim any liability arising directly or indirectly from the use of this book.

We gratefully acknowledge Lucy Davis for her part in overseeing the process and editing our book.

Color by Lennie Peterson

For more information about this book, please contact Boston Post Adoption Resources
at 617.778.6213 or write to marketing@bostonpostadoptionresources.com.

ISBN-13:978-0-692-79787-7
ISBN-10:0-692-79787-4

INTRODUCTION

It has been a dream of ours to write a children's book that simultaneously educates adults. For years, we've wanted to find a way to reach more families touched by adoption and foster care and to create a tool that promotes a broader understanding of post adoption challenges. So often in our practice, we first encounter clients after stress or worry reaches overwhelming levels. As licensed mental health professionals, we've designed *Adoption Is a Lifelong Journey* to proactively provide insight into emotions and thoughts that an adoptee might encounter while also equipping caregivers with timely responses and resources.

Adoption brings its own set of unique experiences of joys and challenges. Our aim is to inform people about these experiences. At Boston Post Adoption Resources (BPAR), we know that no two individuals are the same and everyone's story is different, so what may be difficult for one person may not be a challenge for someone else. However, *Adoption Is a Lifelong Journey* highlights common themes we have seen in our work with families touched by adoption.

This book is written from the perspective of the child, who is often misunderstood or unheard. The child's perspective gives adults a chance to hear what the child may want to say but may not know how to communicate. At times when a child is emotionally overwhelmed his or her behaviors may feel out of control and confusing. We hope our book can offer some insight into the reasons behind the behaviors.

We've designed the first part of *Adoption Is a Lifelong Journey* as a resource adults can read with children to help them connect with their own feelings in an effective, healing way. Through words and illustrations, we aim to provide a sense of safety, security, and assurance that the child is not alone.

This book is intended for any prospective adoptive parents, current adoptive parents, foster parents, adoptees, educators, mental health professionals, families, and anyone interested in learning more about our experience in working with those touched by adoption. We hope it touches your heart the way our work touches ours.

Throughout the book you will notice small puzzle pieces. These link to an expansion of the topic including things to think about, recommendations and resources. You will find these expansions at the back of the book in the "Putting the Pieces Together" section starting on page 18. At Boston Post Adoption Resources it is our nonprofit mission to support and provide resources to anyone touched by adoption. We hope you find these helpful!

Kelly DiBenedetto, LMHC, ATR
Jennifer Eckert, LICSW
Katie Gorczyca, M.A.

This book is dedicated to all of the
amazing individuals and families touched by
adoption that we are privileged to work with
every day! Thank you for inspiring us.

To our colleagues and families,
thank you for your support and encouragement
through our journey of writing.

The Boston Post Adoption Resources (BPAR) team believes in the power of
maintenance, as coming regularly to therapy strengthens the skills
to manage difficulties that may arise in everyday life.

To learn more about our nonprofit mission and services,
please contact us at BPAR.org.

Boston Post Adoption Resources
235 Cypress Street Suite 310
Brookline, MA 02445
617.778.6213
www.bpar.org

Adoption is a lifelong journey.
It means different things to me
at different times.
Sometimes it is just a part of who I am.
Other times it is something
I am actively going through.

I've just begun a new journey with new people, places, smells, and sounds. I could be scared, and I might need some time to settle into this new world. Help me by keeping items from my early beginnings.

2

It might take me a long time to give you the hug you are expecting, but that doesn't mean I don't want it or need it. Help me find different ways of connecting, like shaking hands, high fives, or hand squeezes.

3

I've already had so many goodbyes in my life, and a lot of times I think it is going to happen again. I might test you to see if you will be another goodbye.

Sometimes I can feel like I wasn't meant to be here. Help me remember that, despite my beginnings, I am supposed to be here and there is a reason I am here.

Start talking about my birth family from the beginning, so I know it is always safe to ask and talk about them.

Tell me my adoption story. Protect me by sharing pieces of my birth family and beginnings only as I am able to understand them. Share my information in a way that makes me feel safe.

When you talk about my birth family, it is a reflection of me. If you think that my birth family is "bad," then I may think that a part of me is "bad."

Even though my birth family
couldn't care for me,
it doesn't mean I wasn't loved.

At home and at school, my family history is going to come up. Prepare me. Teach me how to talk to friends, family and other adults, how to answer questions, and how to say no when I want to keep something private.

Connect me with other people
who have been adopted.
I want to know other people who have
experienced what I've been through.

Help me be around others who look like me. Teach me about the culture I came from and let's celebrate it together.

I know the ways that I am like you,
but I might also be wondering about the
parts that come from my birth family
as I develop my own identity.

If people hurt me before I met you,
I might feel really unsafe and out of
control. If you have tried everything to
keep me safe but it isn't working,
it's okay to ask for professional help.

I've noticed that some days
can be harder than others.
I might not be able to say it clearly,
but holidays, birthdays, and transitions
can be hard for me.

Remember to take care of yourself!
By taking care of *you*, you take care of *me*.
I may not understand this at the time,
but I will appreciate it as I grow older.

Adoption is a lifelong journey.
Sometimes it is your journey
and sometimes it is mine,
but no matter what,
it will always be ours.
Let's go through it
and grow through it
together.

Putting the Pieces Together
Key Insights for Caregivers and Loved Ones

Compiled by the Team at Boston Post Adoption Resources (BPAR)

Each puzzle piece corresponds to a page in the front section of the book. Our team of licensed mental health professionals shares corresponding insights, recommendations, and resources for parents and other caregivers or loved ones.

I've just begun a new journey with new people, places, smells, and sounds. I could be scared, and I might need some time to settle into this new world. Help me by keeping items from my early beginnings.

Things to Think About:
When a child first joins a family, everything is new to him or her. Be sensitive to the change in culture: new smells, sounds, faces, languages and rules. If your child comes into the home with clothes or items from his or her birth family or country of origin, take good care of these keepsakes and store them in a safe place where your child can access them and always treasure those pieces of his or her identity.

Recommended Activity:
Create a lifebook containing photographs, artwork, words and any other memorabilia that are important to your child's life. This tool can help your child integrate past experiences with present circumstances, and it's something he or she can treasure forever. This activity is a great way for the adoptive parents and child to normalize adoption, create an openness about adoption, and provide space for the child to discuss and explore his or her feelings about it.

You can adapt the lifebook to any age in order to help your child have a clear understanding of his or her adoption story:

- Adoptive parents and child can create a lifebook together. If the child is very young, the parents fill in the details and the child chooses colors and decorations.
- Adoptive parents can create a lifebook for the young adopted child and present it as a gift to the child as a way to illustrate his or her early beginnings.
- Adoptive parents of teens can outline their own history in a lifebook. This can give the teen a tangible tool when entering a new family.
- Once the lifebook is created, families and children can reference and read it as a way of remembering a child's beginnings.

Recommended Resources:
- *Lifebooks: Creating a Treasure for the Adopted Child* by Beth O'Malley, M.Ed.
- www.adoptionlifebooks.com

It might take me a long time to give you the hug you are expecting, but that doesn't mean I don't want it or need it. Help me find different ways of connecting, like shaking hands, high fives, or hand squeezes.

Things to Think About:
As a new family forms, everyone involved goes through a natural adjustment period. Depending on the circumstances around the adoption, it may take some children longer than others to feel comfortable, safe and secure in the new home. It is important for parents to be aware of their own feelings and expectations about intimacy and connection, and to understand that a child's readiness to connect physically may depend on the cultural norms of his or her birth country. Many parents have waited years for an adoption to occur and have most likely suffered a loss through infertility or other adoptions that did not go through. It's natural to be excited and hopeful. However, children who have experienced trauma may be scared of physical connection and may need a lot of time to build up to a hug or kiss. It's common for parents to feel rejected or disappointed if they aren't able to physically connect with their child right away. If this does occur, it is important for parents to get support from a friend or counselor so they can manage these intense feelings and not let them build up to create a divide between themselves and their child.

Recommended Activity:
It's key to make the transition to the new home as contained and manageable as possible. Focus your efforts on building your family's connection and making sure all family members have the space to share their feelings. Plan to take time off from work, figure out routines that meet your child's needs, set aside time just for play (remember that's how kids learn!), and spend time getting to know each other and developing the culture of your family. Depending on how your child is adjusting to the family, it might make sense to limit visits with extended family members until your child feels comfortable.

Recommended Resources:
- *The Primal Wound: Understanding the Adopted Child* by Nancy Newton Verrier
- *The Connected Child: Bring Hope and Healing to Your Adoptive Family* by Karyn B. Purvis, Ph.D., David R. Cross, Ph.D., and Wendy Lyons Sunshine

**I've already had so many goodbyes in my life,
and a lot of times I think it is going to happen again.
I might test you to see if you will be another goodbye.**

Things to Think About:

Everyone in the adoption triad suffers loss and that sense of loss can be profound. Children who have been removed from their homes and placed into foster care can face multiple placements or might be separated from their siblings. In international adoptions, many children are placed in orphanages where they are left feeling scared and confused. Because many adoptees have had to constantly be prepared for another move, they may find it difficult to truly believe that their new "forever home" is going to be a long-term, safe placement.

For many adoptees, building trust is a slow process. Children will often test their adoptive parents to see if they will leave them. It is also common to see adopted children who feel the need to act perfectly at all times. They may fear that their parents will reject them if they show any sort of fault or imperfection.

Recommended Activity:

If parents anticipate that their child may have a hard time adjusting, they can plan ahead and learn strategies for responding. It's important for parents to have a deep understanding of what their child might be feeling so that they can keep their own reactions and thoughts in check. Help your child express his or her feelings of loss and distrust. Your goal is to let your child feel heard, loved and understood.

Recommended Resources:

- *20 Things Adoptive Parents Need to Succeed* by Sherrie Eldridge
- *The Explosive Child* by Ross W. Greene, Ph.D.
- *Building the Bonds of Attachment* by Daniel A. Hughes

**Sometimes I can feel like I wasn't meant to be here.
Help me remember that, despite my beginnings,
I am supposed to be here and there is a reason I am here.**

Things to Think About:
Although they may not verbalize it, many adopted children question their worth. They might think they were a mistake, that they are bad, or that there is something wrong with them. It's important for parents to reassure their child that he or she is meant to be here and also is meant to be a part of the family. Explain how each of us enters the world in different ways and how families form in different ways: marriage, divorce, stepfamily, birth, adoption, fostering, etc. Make sure your child understands the quality of a family is not measured by how it is formed, but by how the family members value and take care of each other. How we enter the world does not dictate where we are able to go and does not limit what we are able to achieve.

Recommendations:
Self-worth is a complicated concept which often has many different feelings attached to it. Religion or spirituality might provide a useful framework for exploring these concepts. Another suggestion is to talk about fate. Adoptees don't get to choose their beginnings, but they can choose how they want to think about the reason they are here and to believe that each of us has a purpose. Don't underestimate the power of love. Although it can't fix everything, a loving, safe environment can strengthen self-worth and help adoptees feel like they belong, which in turn can lead to a healthy life.

Recommended Resource:

- *A Chance in the World* by Steve Pemberton

Tell me my adoption story. Protect me by sharing pieces of my birth family and beginnings only as I am able to understand them. Share my information in a way that makes me feel safe.

Things to Think About:

It is important that your child knows his or her adoption story. Present the story in a way that is understandable and clear to your child, as well as neutral and fact-based. Since some pieces of the story may be difficult to understand in the beginning, find ways to reframe and explain the story in an age-appropriate manner. Children may ask questions as they grow older and are able to grasp more abstract concepts. Continue to answer truthfully and simply. As your child grows and develops, the story may become more abstract and more detailed, but the message and facts should remain the same.

Recommended Reframes:

Here are two examples of how to describe a child's experience as positive or neutral:

- If your child was placed at a police station, busy street, hospital or other lively area, then the birth parent was most likely hoping for the child to be found in the safest place possible, resulting in immediate care.
- Was the birth family struggling with addiction, substance abuse, or another mental health issue? If they could not take care of themselves, then it would be very challenging for them to take care of someone else.

Recommended Resources:

- *Telling the Truth to Your Adopted or Foster Child: Making Sense of the Past (2nd edition)* by Betsy Keefer Smalley and Jayne E. Schooler
- *Tell Me a Real Adoption Story* by Betty Jean Lifton, illustrated by Claire A. Nivola

**When you talk about my birth family, it is a reflection of me.
If you think that my birth family is "bad,"
then I may think that a part of me is "bad."**

Things to Think About:

Children's feelings about their birth family can be quite complicated and can vary depending on their experiences and memories. Children know they are a part of their birth family even though they live apart. Give them the space to figure out their own feelings towards their birth family, and recognize that these feelings may change over time. For children who were abused or neglected by their birth family, explain how their situation was unsafe so they understand why they were removed.

Recommendations for Conversations:

Adoptees want to know they came from somewhere good, so it is incredibly important that adoptive parents don't make negative statements about birth parents. At times this can be extremely challenging, especially if there was neglect or abuse. If it's difficult to come up with positive language about the birth family, then stay neutral. The following language tips can be helpful:

- Acknowledge and respect that pain and loss were an early part of the relationship. For example, parents might say, "We have no control over how we enter the world or our earliest beginnings, however we do have control over the way we choose to live our lives. We choose love and acceptance in our family."

- Stay away from these words: abandoned, unwanted, given up, unloved, lucky.

- If your child expresses anger or resentment towards his or her birth parents, validate those feelings. If your child's birth parents did hurt him or her, it's important and productive to allow your child to acknowledge powerful emotions about the experience.

- Help your child find healthy ways of expressing anger and prepare him or her for the impact that this might have on other relationships in life.

Recommended Resources:
- *Coming Home to Self: Healing the Primal Wound* by Nancy Newton Verrier
- *I Wish for You a Beautiful Life* edited by Sara Dorow, introduction by Mrs. Han Sang-soon

At home and at school, my family history is going to come up. Prepare me. Teach me how to talk to friends, family and other adults, how to answer questions, and how to say no when I want to keep something private.

Things to Think About:

School and extracurricular activities are very likely to bring up a child's family history. What may seem straightforward to non-adoptive families can spark a lot of questions for a child who is adopted. Assignments to draw a family tree, to bring in a photograph of when the child was a baby, and to explore and study genetics can all produce a number of reactions to an adopted child, such as anxiety, fear, sadness, and anger. Friends may ask questions with good intentions, but it can feel overwhelming to a child who is adopted.

Recommendations:

Discuss strategies in advance so your child feels confident when approached with questions about his or her adoption. Remind your child that he or she has choices and never has to answer an adoption question if he or she does not want to. Your child also has the ability to educate other children or teachers about adoption in general, which can boost a child's confidence. You can reinforce your child's efforts by being proactive at parent-teacher conferences and other meetings.

Recommended Resources:

- *W.I.S.E. UP! Powerbook* written by Marilyn Schoettle, M.A.
- *In On It: What Adoptive Parents Would Like You to Know About Adoption* by Elisabeth O'Toole
- *Adoption and the Schools: Resources for Parents and Teachers* edited by Lansing Wood and Nancy Ng, www.fairfamilies.org
- www.adoptionsupport.org

Connect me with other people who have been adopted. I want to know other people who have experienced what I've been through. Help me be around others who look like me. Teach me about the culture I came from and let's celebrate it together. I know the ways that I am like you, but I might also be wondering about the parts that come from my birth family as I develop my own identity.

Things to Think About:
It's extremely important to help your child feel connected to and understood by others. Your child needs to spend time with other adoptees so he or she has access to people who have gone through a similar experience. The concept of identity for an adoptee is complex. Many adoptees, particularly international adoptees, have very limited or no information at all about their beginnings. They can experience a profound sense of loss around the unknown, and the unanswered questions of their history. The beginning narrative of an adoptee's life, whether it is known or unknown, has a very large impact on identity.

Identity:
Every teenager goes through a normative crisis of identity development. However, for adoptees, this crisis begins earlier and can ebb and flow throughout life. Adoptees often have many questions about who they look like, why they were placed for adoption, whether or not their birth mothers think about them, and how their lives might have been different if they hadn't been adopted. For some adoptees, this identity exploration may lead to a desire to search for birth family, a complicated and emotional process. Consider seeking professional support during this process.

Race:
For transracial adoptions, do acknowledge racial differences within the family. Allow the child or teenager to feel safe discussing his or her racial identity and feelings about it. Recognize that your family is now a multicultural family. Parents should educate their children about racism, stereotypes, and oppression so that they are prepared for questions and experiences from others. Parents should be aware of racial identity development so that they can help their children throughout the various stages of this complex and important experience. Embrace living in a diverse community and integrate other multicultural families into your life. Your child needs direct involvement with experiences and individuals from his or her birth culture and race in order to fully understand and feel connected to it. The goal is to help your child feel connected to and secure in his or her racial identity and birth culture.

Recommendations:

There are many proactive things that parents can do to help, including living in a diverse community. Connect with one of the many adoption community organizations and try attending support groups for kids, teenagers or adults. For children who have come from a particularly strong religious or cultural background, help them stay connected by joining a religious organization, or encourage them to attend a heritage camp. The best thing you can do for your child is to provide an open and understanding environment for exploring all areas of identity, including gender and sexuality. Keep the lines of communication open and access many of the excellent resources below to further educate yourself.

Recommended Resources:

- *The Harris Narratives: An Introspective Study of a Transracial Adoptee* by Susan Harris O'Connor

- *Being Adopted: The Lifelong Search for Self* by David M. Brodzinsky, Ph.D, Marshall D. Schechter, M.D. and Robin Marantz Henig

- *Beneath the Mask: Understanding Adopted Teens* by Debbie Riley, M.S., and John Meeks, M.D.

- *Birthright: The Guide to Search and Reunion for Adoptees, Birthparents, and Adoptive Parents* by Jean A. S. Strauss

- *Building Self-Esteem in Children and Teens Who Are Adopted or Fostered* by Dr. Sue Cornbluth

If people hurt me before I met you, I might feel really unsafe and out of control. If you have tried everything to keep me safe but it isn't working, it's okay to ask for professional help.

Things to Think About:

Many individuals who are adopted have experienced trauma, and all have experienced loss. If your child has experienced a trauma and is struggling, it's critical to get him or her support early so that he or she can develop coping skills, healthy attachment patterns, and a healthy identity. If a child is unable to engage in daily activities, routines, or is physically and emotionally out of control, seek professional help. Options might include consulting with your pediatrician, individual therapy, or family therapy. Find a clinician with expertise in adoption, as it is a unique experience.

Recommended Resources:

- *Trauma and Recovery* by Judith Herman, M.D.
- *Adoption Healing...A Path to Recovery* by Joe Soll, LCSW
- *Parenting the Hurt Child: Helping Adoptive Families Heal and Grow* by Gregory C. Keck, Ph.D. and Regina M. Kupecky, LSW
- www.bpar.org

Remember to take care of yourself! By taking care of *you*, you take care of *me*. I may not understand this at the time, but I will appreciate it as I grow older.

Things to Think About:
When we have so much to look after and take care of, we often forget to take care of ourselves. Remember to listen to your own needs, especially when a child enters your life. It may seem counterintuitive, but taking time for yourself will help you be more present, aware, and attentive as a parent.

Recommendations:
Regular exercise, meditation, journaling, play groups to meet other parents, positive self-talk, and professionals such as psychologists, social workers, clergy, support groups, school guidance, pediatricians and other doctors are some suggestions for self-care and support. These professional supports can provide skills and suggestions specific to your needs, even at the preventative level before any challenges develop.

Recommended Resources:
- *The Art of Extreme Self-Care: Transform Your Life One Month at a Time* by Cheryl Richardson
- *Simple Abundance: A Daybook of Comfort and Joy* by Sarah Ban Breathnach
- *Gift from the Sea* by Anne Morrow Lindbergh
- The BPAR blog at www.bpar.org

Notes and Thoughts

CPSIA information can be obtained
at www.ICGtesting.com
Printed in the USA
LVHW071543010519
616261LV00002B/31/P